# Tag, You're It!

## 101 Tag Games
### for
## Fun, Fitness, and Skills

## Guy Bailey

**Educators Press**
Vancouver, Washington

ISBN: 978-0-9669727-9-5

**Publisher's Cataloging-in-Publication**
*(Provided by Quality Books, Inc.)*

Bailey, Guy, 1956-
   Tag, you're it! : 101 tag games for fun, fitness and
skills / Guy Bailey.
   pages cm
   LCCN 2013948135
   ISBN 9780966972795

   1. Tag games.   I. Title.

GV1207.B34 2013                796.1'4
                               QBI13-600150

.

The author and publisher assume that the reader will teach these games using professional judgment and respect for student safety. In regards to this statement, the author and publisher shall have neither liability nor responsibility in the case of injury to anyone participating in the activities contained within.

# EDUCATORS PRESS
**15610 NE 8th Street**
**Vancouver, WA  98684**
**(360) 597-4355**
**www.educatorspress.com**

**Printed in the United States of America**

# Acknowledgments

Many thanks go out to all of my colleagues in the physical education profession. Because some of the game ideas contained in this resource have been collected from attending workshops and conventions for almost three decades, it's impossible to give specific game credit. However, I have learned so much from you through the sharing of our game ideas and teaching methodology.

Special thanks to my wonderful students at Concord, Spring Mountain, and Sunnyside Elementary Schools who voluntarily played all of these games. I would have had few opportunities to modify and create these game ideas without them. Their exuberance for physical education and game playing was a constant source of inspiration and encouragement.

Thanks also to all of the administrators, staff, and friends that make up the North Clackamas School District in Milwaukie, Oregon. It's been a blessing and an honor to work with all of you. The families in this community are fortunate to have a school board and administrative team that truly value physical education and its many contributions to the overall education of children.

I would also like to acknowledge the many talented professionals that contributed to the design and production of this book. I am particularly indebted to Olga Melnik for her outstanding illustrations.

Finally, an author's family is always owed the greatest amount of gratitude, for they are the ones who truly make the biggest sacrifices. A special "Thank you!" goes to my wife, Paula, for her understanding, encouragement, and support.

# About the Author

Guy Bailey, M.ED., has over 30 years of experience teaching physical education at the elementary and middle school levels. He currently teaches elementary physical education in the North Clackamas School District which is located in Milwaukie, Oregon. During this time, he has also directed many after-school sport activities and coached numerous youth sports. His educational background includes having a B.S. degree (Central Washington University) and a M.Ed. degree (Portland State University) in his specialty area of physical education.

In addition to this title, Guy has authored five other books in the area of physical education. *The Physical Educator's Big Book of Sport Lead-Up Games* (2003) is widely considered the most comprehensive resource of games used to develop sport skills ever published. His popular book, *Recess Success* (2007), is a special collection of more than 200 playground and recess games for the elementary school. It is a revised and updated version of *The Ultimate Playground & Recess Game Book,* a book he originally authored in 2001. *The Ultimate Homeschool Physical Education Game Book* (2004) is a unique resource aimed at helping home schooling families teach physical education skills in the home and backyard setting. In 2007, Guy authored *Gym Scooter Fun & Games*, the first book ever published on the subject of gym scooter games and activities. In 2013, he authored *201 Small-Sided Sports & Games*, a one-of-a-kind resource devoted to game activities that maximize participation and skill development.

As a physical educator, Guy's goal is to equip each of his students with a wide range of movement skills coupled with a love of being physical active. He believes that *lasting* skill learning in physical education needs to consist of success-oriented experiences that literally leave children craving for more. His books reflect this philosophy of using learning activities that are both skill based and fun.

Guy and his wife, Paula, reside in Vancouver, Washington and Surprise, Arizona. He has four children—Justin, Austin, Carson, and Heather. Guy enjoys family time together, exercising, writing, hiking the mountains of Oregon and Arizona, and attending PAC-12 intercollegiate sporting events in the Pacific Northwest and Arizona.

# Preface

Tag games have been around for generations. They are simple, easy to organize, and they contain the necessary element of fun which is always a motivator of exercise for children. However, not all are non-elimination, safe, or contain specific skill outcomes that make them suitable for the school and recreational setting. The intention of this resource is to provide you with a large selection of games to get elementary-age children genuinely excited about physical education participation while developing specific movement, fitness, academic, dance, and sport skills. These unique games are designed for maximum involvement by all players where everybody is playing 100% all of the time. This is no exclusion or elimination of players. In fact, the enhancement of cardiovascular health is a benefit of each of these field-tested games. All of these simple, but versatile, activities has been used successfully with my students and has proven to be fun and enjoyable game experiences.

In all, there are 101 tag games included in this carefully chosen collection to meet the needs of a wide variety of ages and skill levels. There are fitness-building games, academic games, dance-type games, character-building games, and games for groups of all sizes. In choosing the games for this book, I purposely left out those that take an excessive amount of time to set up and/or explain to children. It's my philosophy that the more time in class children are physically active, the better. I have used all of these games as quick warm-up activities or as instant starters with great success. They also make for terrific activities to end a lesson or for reviewing skills at any time during a lesson.

To help you navigate the book, the games are listed alphabetically with the exception that the dance-related and partner tag games are grouped together toward the end of the book. Each game provides everything for its successful use, including an introduction with a skill purpose, equipment needed, and easy-to-understand play instructions. In addition, I have included instructional suggestions and safety guidelines on using tag games in any play setting. For school professionals, you can read each game's introduction to help guide you through the game selection process since every game enhances children's cognitive, social/emotional, and physical development.

All of us have heard of the often reported studies showing an increase in childhood obesity. It's imperative that children develop healthier lifestyles, which will involve being physically active more often. It's my hope that using these games will meet that need for increased physical activity. It's also my desire that these fun-packed games will foster a positive attitude toward physical education and movement that is lasting—and, will leave your students asking to play again and again.

As someone who has taught physical education for more than 30 years and is always looking for new and fun ways to provide quality learning experiences, I trust you'll find *Tag, Your It!* to be a much-used resource. Have fun!

# Guidelines for Safe and Effective Game Playing

Once you have chosen a tag game that meets your desired instructional objective, it is time to present it to the children. The following instructional procedures will enhance your presentation of the game while ensuring the safety of children.

- Before introducing tag games, teach children how to move in general space and in various directions. Practice traveling by looking in the direction one is going, avoiding collisions, staying away from walls and other obstacles.

- All tag games should be limited to jogging or a movement pattern (such as skipping or walking) *other than running*. Moving safely is imperative. Model to the students the proper and safe speed of a slow jog or walk before the start of a game.

- Unless one of the games states otherwise, a good rule of thumb is to use one tagger for every five people playing. For example, there would be five taggers for a group of twenty-five players.

- Always identify the taggers with vests, arm bands, or an object such as holding a foam ball.

- The instructor should discuss safety precautions at the beginning of each new game.

- Use only foam balls when games call for the use of such objects.

- Before play begins, ensure that students have a sufficient understanding of the rules.

- Monitor players for fatigue constantly.

- Use consistent starting and stopping signals.

- For instructors, know your students and gain an understanding of their maturity, skill level, and experience when choosing a game activity.

- Establish boundaries and identify safety hazards.

- Keep the play area free of obstacles and make sure floors are completely dry.

- Make sure everyone is properly dressed for movement. Require athletic shoes.

# Contents

# Addition Tag

**Introduction:** This fun activity is a terrific lead-in to beginning math skills for younger players. It also develops cardiovascular health.

**Equipment:** None

**How to Play:** Select two pairs of players to start out as the "It" players. Each "It" pair starts out holding hands. The other players start anywhere throughout the play area.

On a starting signal, the "It" pairs attempt to tag the other players. A tagged player must join hands with the "It"—and each subsequent tagged player also joins hands with the growing It. However, once an "It" has grown to four players, the group divides in the middle to form two separate "Its" (that is, two players in each "It"). Each subsequent "It" splits again once it has four players. If the "It" breaks or must stop for any reason, then the chained players have to reconnect before resuming.

Play is continuous until all players are part of an "It."

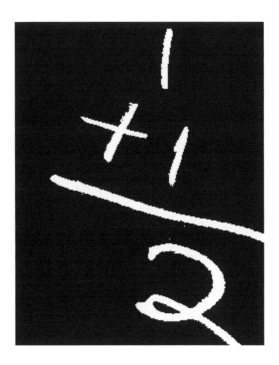

# Alphabet Tag

**Introduction:** Here is a great activity that mixes lots of healthy movement with language arts.

**Equipment:** Foam balls or identification vests for the taggers

**How to Play:** Before play, review the shapes of letters that the players have previously learned.

Select players to be the chasers and hand each one a foam ball or an identification vest for tagging.

On a starting signal, the chasers attempt to tag the other players. Once tagged, the player immediately freezes in a standing position and creates the shape of a letter of the alphabet. Frozen players are not allowed to lie down to form a letter as this would be unsafe (they could be stepped and/or someone could trip over them). A free player can rescue a tagged player by standing directly in front of him/her, and successfully naming the correct letter. If the guess is incorrect, the tagged player can then give "clues" until the correct answer is given. Players cannot be tagged while rescuing others.

A variation for the older players would be have the frozen players form a previously chosen letter that everyone would assume if caught—but, now the rescuers ask them to come up with a word that begins with that letter. If successful, the tagged player is back in the game. For example, if the letter of the day is "A," then a correct word would be "apple."

Play is continuous until time is called.

# Amoeba Tag

**Introduction:** This game is one of my favorites as it keeps everyone moving and engaged. Before play, discuss the organism called the Amoeba and how it makes new cells by dividing in half.

**Equipment:** None

**How to Play:** Select three players to start out as Amoeba players. To form an Amoeba, the three players join hands. The other players start anywhere throughout the play area.

On a starting signal, the Amoeba attempts to tag the other players. A tagged player must join hands with the Amoeba—and each subsequent tagged player also joins hands with the growing Amoeba. However, once an Amoeba has grown to six players, it divides in the middle to form two Amoebas. Each subsequent Amoeba splits again once it has six players. Only the ends of the Amoeba can make tags. If the Amoeba breaks or must stop for any reason, then the chained players have to reconnect before resuming.

Play is continuous until all players are part of an Amoeba.

# Arch Tag

**Introduction:** Here is a fun game that maximizes participation and is a great choice for developing aerobic endurance and cooperation.

**Equipment:** Identification vests for the chasers

**How to Play:** Select two or three pairs of players to start out as the chasers and have them wear vests for identification.

Before play, have all participants form pairs. Each player holds hands or wrists with their partner. On a starting signal, the chasers attempt to tag the other pairs. Once a pair is tagged, the two players must form an "arch" by facing each other with the hands joined overhead. Other pairs being chased can free those caught by running through the arch.

Play is continuous until time is called or until all pairs are caught and forming arches.

# Astronaut Tag

**Introduction:** This chasing and fleeing game develops cardiovascular endurance and allows children to move with imaginary fun.

**Equipment:** Three foam balls or vests for the taggers; three foam balls or vests of a different color for the rescuers

**How to Play:** Select three players to be the taggers (known as the "asteroids") and three players to be the rescuers (known as the "astronauts"). Identify these players with different colored balls or identification vests.

On a starting signal, the taggers ("asteroids") chase and attempt to tag the other players. Players who are tagged must walk around in a dazed and wobbly fashion. Meanwhile, the rescuers ("astronauts") move around and rescue the tagged players by gently touching them on the shoulders. The astronauts can never be tagged by an asteroid.

Play is continuous.

# Balance Tag

**Introduction:** Here is an active tag game that allows children to freeze in a balance position that is both challenging and fun.

**Equipment:** Foam balls or identification vests for the taggers

**How to Play:** Select players to be the chasers and hand each one a foam ball (or wear an identification vest) for tagging.

On a starting signal, the chasers attempt to tag the other players. Once tagged, the player immediately freezes into a balance position by standing one foot and reaching back with a hand to hold the opposite foot. The tagged player should have his/her free hand extended straight forward (see illustration below). A free player can rescue a tagged player by lightly touching the hand that is extended.

Play is continuous until time is called.

# Banana Tag

**Introduction:** Banana Tag incorporates the skill of cooperation with lots of imaginative fun and movement.

**Equipment:** Several player identification vests or foam balls for the taggers

**How to Play:** Select several players to be the chasers and hand each one an identification vest or a foam ball for tagging.

On a starting signal, the chasers attempt to tag the other players. Once tagged, the player freezes in a position like a banana—that is, standing with a slight lean, both feet together, and arms held high with the hands together. The frozen banana player can be freed when two free players grab his/her hands and move the arms down to the banana's sides (as if "unpeeling" the banana). Free players cannot be tagged while performing the unpeeling movement.

Play is continuous. Select new chasers often.

# Barnyard Tag

**Introduction:** Here is an imaginative and active tag game that allows younger children to have fun with animal sound effects.

**Equipment:** Several player identification vests or foam balls for the taggers

**How to Play:** Select several players to be the "Farmers" (the chasers) and hand each one an identification vest or a foam ball for tagging.

On a starting signal, the Farmers attempt to tag the other players. Once tagged, the player immediately gets in a position that resembles the farm animal that he/she wants to depict and also makes the sound of that animal. The tagged animal player can be freed once a free player stands directly in front of him/her and guesses the name of the correct farm animal. No player can be tagged while trying to free an animal.

Play is continuous. Select new chasers often.

# Batman Tag

**Introduction:** This theme type game develops cardiovascular endurance and allows children to participate in an atmosphere of imaginative fun.

**Equipment:** Three or four foam balls or vests for the taggers; two foam balls or vests of a different color for Batman and Robin

**How to Play:** Select three or four players to be the chasers (the Joker, the Penguin, Catwoman, Mr. Freeze, or any of the other rival characters in the Batman movies) and two players to be the rescuers (Batman and Robin). Identify these players with different colored balls or identification vests.

On a starting signal, the Batman "rivals" chase and attempt to tag the other players. Players who are tagged must get down on all fours (hands and feet) and stay in that frozen position. Meanwhile, Batman and Robin move around and rescue the frozen players by gently touching them on the shoulders. Batman and Robin can never be tagged by a Rival.

Play is continuous.

# Beanbag Tag

**Introduction:** This high-energy game allows children to practice the underhand throw with lots of chasing, fleeing, dodging, leaping, and jumping mixed in.

**Equipment:** One beanbag for each player

**How to Play:** All players start with a beanbag in hand and spread out among the play area.

On a starting signal, all players begin moving about the play area and try to tag others by hitting their feet with an underhanded throw of the beanbag (the throw should resemble the rolling motion used in bowling). At the same time, each player is trying to avoid getting hit. Once hit, a player must perform five jumping jacks at that place before resuming play. The objective is to tag as many players as possible and, at the same time, be tagged the least often.

After each toss of the beanbag, players need to retrieve their original beanbag. Also, players can only "tag" others by making contact with another player's foot—no hitting of the body above the foot is allowed.

Play is continuous until time is called.

# Bicycle Tag

**Introduction:** The name of this game is derived from the bicycling movement that a tagged player must perform together with a rescuing player. Besides developing the social skill of cooperation, this game also enhances aerobic fitness.

**Equipment:** Several player identification vests or foam balls for the taggers

**How to Play:** Select several players to be the chasers and hand each one an identification vest or foam ball for tagging.

On a starting signal, the chasers attempt to tag the other players. Once players are tagged, they must lie down on their back with their feet raised. A tagged player can be freed when any free player lies down, places his/her soles (bottom of feet) against the soles of the tagged player, and performs a joint "bicycling" motion for a count of 10 seconds. When finished, both players jump up and rejoin the game. No rescuing player can be tagged while bicycling.

Play is continuous. Select new chasers often.

# Bird Dog Tag

**Introduction:** The name of this game is derived from the position that tagged players must hold once caught and waiting to be rescued. This two-point balance adds to the fun and challenging nature of this high-energy game.

**Equipment:** Several player identification vests or foam balls for the taggers

**How to Play:** Select several players to be the chasers and hand each one an identification vest or foam ball for tagging.

On a starting signal, the chasers attempt to tag the other players. Once a player is tagged, he or she forms a "bird dog" position by assuming a push-up hold with one hand and one foot off the floor. The hand and foot should be from opposite sides of the body. The tagged player can be freed when any free player crawls under him/her. No rescuing player can be tagged while crawling under a bird dog.

Play is continuous. Select new chasers often.

# Bowling Tag

**Introduction:** This active game incorporates the skills of cooperation, rolling a ball, and aerobic endurance.

**Equipment:** Several player identification vests for the taggers; several playground balls for the rescuers

**How to Play:** Before play, review the rolling motion used in bowling. Have players practice with a partner and/or aim at a target (like a bowling pin) to develop proficiency.

Select several players to be the chasers and hand each one an identification vest for tagging. Also select an equal number of rescuers and hand each one a playground ball.

On a starting signal, the chasers attempt to tag the other players. Once tagged, the player freezes in a standing position with both legs spread apart and arms held high. The frozen player can be freed when a rescuer teams up with any free player and the two roll the ball through the legs of the frozen player. The free player catching the rolled ball now becomes the next rescuer and the previously frozen player is now free to move about. Free players cannot be tagged while performing the rolling action with a rescuer.

Play is continuous. Select new chasers often.

# Bridge Tag

**Introduction:** This game, a variation of "Tunnel Tag," is a classic and is played by children around the world. Its name is derived from the position that tagged players must hold once caught and waiting to be freed.

**Equipment:**  Several player identification vests or foam balls for the taggers

**How to Play:**  Select several players to be the chasers and hand each one an identification vest or foam ball for tagging.

On a starting signal, the chasers attempt to tag the other players. Once tagged, the player forms a "bridge" by holding a position on his/her feet and hands. Any type of bridge is acceptable as long as three or more body parts are used for support and another player can crawl under it. The frozen player can be freed any unfrozen player who crawls through his/her bridge. Also, no rescuing player can be tagged while crawling through a bridge

Play is continuous. Select new chasers often.

# Buddy Tag

**Introduction:** This partner game is a great choice as an instant starter and/or for use as a cardiovascular activity during a physical education class.

**Equipment:** None

**How to Play:** Choose 3 or 4 players to start as the taggers. Have the other players partner up and joined together by locking inside elbows or holding hands. Players must stay joined together as they move about the play area.

On a starting signal, each tagger tries to tag the arm or elbow of any of the sets of partners. When the taggers succeed, they join elbows or hold hands with the player they tagged and that player lets go of their old partner—the old player now becomes a tagger. Play continues in this fashion until time is called.

For fair play, do not allow "touchbacks." A touchback is when a player is tagged and then he/she immediately tags back the player who just tagged them.

# Cars Tag

**Introduction:** This imaginative game is a favorite for children in the primary grades. It's also a nice cardiovascular workout since the game is practically non-stop.

**Equipment:** Several same-colored foam balls for the taggers; several differently-colored foam balls for the "Tow Maters"

**How to Play:** Select several players to be the chasers and the same number to be the "Tow Maters." Hand each one a foam ball for tagging (the "Tow Maters" should have a differently colored ball).

On a starting signal, the chasers attempt to tag the other players (who are all "Lightning McQueen Cars"). Once tagged, the car immediately stops, jogs in place, and yells out "Help!" A "Tow Mater" player can fix the broken down car by lightly touching its shoulder and saying "Hit the open road!" The car is now free to drive away.

Play is continuous. Select new chasers and Tow Maters periodically.

# Catch Tag

**Introduction:** Here is a fun chasing and fleeing game that builds endurance and the skills of underhand throwing and catching at the same time.

**Equipment:** Several player identification vests for the taggers; several foam or fleece balls for the rescuers.

**How to Play:** Select several players to be the taggers, and hand each one an identification vest for tagging. Also, select several players to be the beginning rescuers and give each a small foam or fleece ball.

Before play, it's important to review the proper form of executing an underhanded throw and catch.

On a starting signal, the taggers attempt to catch the other players by touching them on the shoulders. Once tagged, players must freeze in a standing position with both hands held high. Any of the players with a ball (the "rescuers") can unfreeze a frozen player by successfully performing an underhanded toss and catch with him/her. The player receiving the throw now moves around and looks for another frozen player to throw and catch with. A dropped ball is available for any free player to pick up.

Play is continuous. Select new taggers often.

# Chain Tag

**Introduction:** Here is a total-participation game that keeps everyone moving and is a great choice for developing aerobic endurance.

**Equipment:** None

**How to Play:** Select three players to start out as "chain" chasers.

On a starting signal, the three chasers attempt to tag the other players. Once tagged, players must join hands with the person making the tag. Each subsequent tagged player also joins hands with the growing "chain." Only the ends of the chain can make tags. If the chain breaks or must stop for any reason, then the chained players have to reconnect before resuming. The objective is to stay free of the three growing chains.

Play is continuous until all players are linked.

# Change-Up Tag

**Introduction:** Here is an aerobic tag game that allows children to have fun with various locomotor movements such as skipping, sliding, jumping, hopping, walking, galloping, and jogging.

**Equipment:** Several player identification vests or foam balls for the taggers

**How to Play:** Select several players to be the chasers and hand each one an identification vest or a foam ball for tagging. Before play, explain all of the various locomotor choices for moving in this game (jogging, walking, skipping, hopping, jumping, sliding, and galloping).

On a starting signal, the chasers attempt to tag the other players who are jogging slowly around the play area. However, tagged players must immediately change the way they move to skipping, sliding, galloping, and so forth. Each additional tag results in the player changing the way he/she moves. Tagged players cannot resume a regular jog unless they have exhausted all of the other locomotor movements first. The objective is to be tagged as few times as possible.

Play is continuous. Select new chasers often.

# Cholesterol Tag

**Introduction:** This is an excellent tag game for developing cardiovascular health and reinforcing the health principles behind blood cholesterol. Studies have proven a direct link behind healthy habits, such as exercise and diet, and our ratio of LDL (the bad cholesterol) and HDL (the good cholesterol).

**Equipment:** Several yellow foam balls for the "LDL" taggers; several foam balls of a different color for the rescuing "Cardiologists"

**How to Play:** Before play, explain the importance of making smart food choices and exercising daily and how it relates to our cholesterol level. Also review the difference between LDL and HDL cholesterol, and explain how healthy habits (such as exercise) can lower the bad cholesterol (LDL) and raise the good cholesterol (HDL).

Select several players to be the "LDL Taggers," and hand each one a yellow foam ball for tagging. Also select several players to begin as rescuing "Cardiologists" and hand each a foam ball of a different color other than yellow. The yellow balls represent the build-up of the bad cholesterol.

On a starting signal, the LDL Taggers attempt to tag the other players. Once tagged, players freeze in a standing position with a hand held high. They have to hold this position until a rescuing Cardiologist comes by and says "I'm prescribing EXERCISE!" After mirroring together an exercise (of the cardiologist choosing) for 5-10 seconds, the tagged player is then free to move about. Cardiologists can never be tagged.

Play is continuous. Select new LDL Taggers and Cardiologists often.

# Circle Tag

**Introduction:** This fast-moving game will raise players' heart rates for enhancing cardio-vascular health and lateral movement. It also requires everyone to work together in an atmosphere of cooperation.

**Equipment:** None

**How to Play:** Organize the players into individual groups of four. Three players join hands and form a circle; the fourth player, who is outside of the circle, is the "It."

The game begins with the "It" announcing who he/she will try to tag. The players in the circle work together (with hands joined at all times) by sliding laterally to the right or left to prevent that player from being tagged by the "It." The "It" cannot reach over or under the circle to make a tag—he/she can only attempt a tag by moving around the outside of the circle. When the "It" tags the player, the two change roles.

For fair play, emphasize to each circle that they must move sideways in a circular fashion in one spot to avoid a tag and not run as a group around the play area.

# Compliment Tag

**Introduction:** Here is a game that works great as a warm-up activity in a physical education class. It also sets a positive tone for children as everyone loves to be complimented!

**Equipment:** Several foam balls or identification vests for the taggers

**How to Play:** Before play, review the concept of a compliment and give examples.

Select several players to be the chasers and hand each one a foam ball (or wear an identification vest) for tagging.

On a starting signal, the chasers attempt to tag the other players. Once tagged, players immediately freeze in a standing position with one hand held high. A free player can unfreeze a frozen player by giving him/her a compliment (for example, "you have a great sense of humor and make me laugh!"). Both players then "high five" each other and rejoin the game.

Play is continuous until time is called. Choose new taggers periodically.

# Crab Tag

**Introduction:** This is an excellent tag game for building muscular strength and endurance. It's also an ideal choice for play areas where space is limited.

**Equipment:** Several identification vests for the taggers

**How to Play:** Before play, review the proper execution of the "crab walk." This is having hands and feet on the floor while facing upward (that is, an "upside down push-up" type of position), and moving either forward or backward while maintaining this position.

Select several players to be the "Taggers," and hand each identification vest. All players start scattered about in the play area in a crab position.

On a starting signal, the crab taggers attempt to tag the other players (who are also crab walking). Once tagged, players turn around and freeze in the "up" push-up position. They have to hold this position until a free crab comes along and crawls under them. When finished, both players resume crab walking and are free to move around. Rescuing crabs can never be tagged.

Play is continuous. Select new chasers often.

# Crazy Eights Tag

**Introduction:** This active game incorporates jogging with a crawling movement that resembles the number eight. For younger players, it is important to demonstrate the correct form used in making the number eight prior to playing the game.

**Equipment:** Several player identification vests or foam balls for the taggers

**How to Play:** Select several players to be the chasers and hand each one an identification vest or a foam ball for tagging.

On a starting signal, the chasers attempt to tag the other players. Once tagged, players have to stand in a stationary position with the legs spread apart and arms crossed. Free players can rescue tagged players by crawling under their legs in a figure eight pattern, and finishing with a high-ten (both players clapping hands together). No player can be tagged while performing the figure eight movement.

Play is continuous. Select new chasers often.

# Dental Health Tag

**Introduction:** This is an excellent tag game for developing cardiovascular health while enhancing the principles of dental health—in this case, reinforcing the importance of brushing regularly for healthy teeth.

**Equipment:** Several yellow foam balls for the "Plaque" taggers; several pool noodles (the "toothbrushes") for the rescuing "Dentists"

**How to Play:** Before play, explain how yellowing plaque can accumulate on teeth and cause cavities when teeth are not brushed regularly.

Select several players to be the "Plaque Taggers," and hand each one a yellow foam ball for tagging. Also select several players to begin as rescuing "Dentists" and hand each a pool noodle. The pool noodles represent the toothbrushes.

On a starting signal, the Plaque Taggers attempt to tag the other players. Once tagged, players freeze in a standing position with a hand held high. They have to hold this position until a rescuing Dentist comes by and gently brushes the tagged player's shoulder (with the "toothbrush") to get rid of his or her "plaque." After a few seconds of "brushing," the tagged player is now free to move about. Dentists can never be tagged.

Play is continuous. Select new Plaque Taggers and Dentists often.

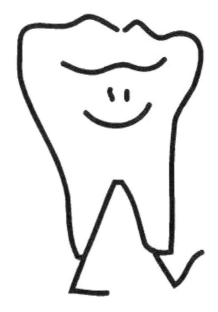

# Dishrag Tag

**Introduction:** Here is a terrific game that requires cooperation and lots of healthy movement.

**Equipment:** Foam balls or identification vests for the taggers

**How to Play:** Select several players to be the chasers and hand each one a foam ball (or wear an identification vest) for tagging.

On a starting signal, the chasers attempt to tag the other players. Once tagged, the player immediately freezes in a motionless position with both arms held high in the air. A free player can rescue a tagged player by standing directly in front of him/her, joining hands, and then turning (in the same direction) under the arms in a full turn back to the original starting position. Once completed, both players shake hands and the tagged player is now free. No free player can be tagged while trying to rescue someone.

Play is continuous until time is called.

# Everybody's It

**Introduction:** This could also be called the "fastest tag game in the world!" It's an excellent choice for a quick warm-up or instant activity in a physical education class or recreational setting.

**Equipment:** None

**How to Play:** All players start in their own personal space and spread out among the play area. All players are taggers, and every player can tag every other player.

On a starting signal, all players attempt to run from each other while trying to tag other players. Once a player is frozen, he or she stands in a stationary position with one hand held high, and eyes on the player who tagged him or her. A frozen player is free to return to the game once the player who originally tagged him/her is tagged (this is why it's important to watch the tagger after he/she leaves and moves on).

As a safety precaution, require all players to use a movement other than jogging or running (sliding and skipping are ideal).

Play is continuous until time is called.

# Extraterrestrial Tag

**Introduction:** This fun game incorporates imagination with lots of healthy movement.

**Equipment:** Several player identification vests or foam balls for the taggers

**How to Play:** Select several players to be the chasers (the "NASA officials") and hand each one an identification vest or a foam ball for tagging.

On a starting signal, the chasers ("NASA officials") attempt to tag the other players (who are free ET's). Once tagged, the player freezes in a stationary position with his/her index finger held in the air. In order to get unfrozen, another player (a free ET) must put his/her index finger against the frozen player's index finger and say the words, "ET phone home!" Players cannot be tagged while performing the rescuing act.

Play is continuous. Select new chasers often.

# Favorite Tag

**Introduction:** This game allows children the fun of sharing their favorite things with others while getting lots of healthy movement!

**Equipment:** Several player identification vests or foam balls for the taggers

**How to Play:** Select several players to be the chasers and hand each one an identification vest or a foam ball for tagging.

Before play, select a "favorite" category for the players to share during the game. Examples include books, toys, sports, school subjects, colors, fruits, etc.

On a starting signal, the chasers attempt to tag the other players. Once tagged, the player stands stationary with one hand held high. The tagged player can be freed once a free player stands directly in front of him/her and both share their favorite thing (in the previously selected category). Once both have shared, they "high-five" each other and continue playing. No player can be tagged while sharing.

Play is continuous. Select new chasers often.

# First Aid Tag

**Introduction:** This non-stop imaginative game enhances cardiovascular health. It also reinforces the first aid principle of applying direct pressure to a wound.

**Equipment:** Player identification vests or foam balls for the taggers (enough for about half of the players)

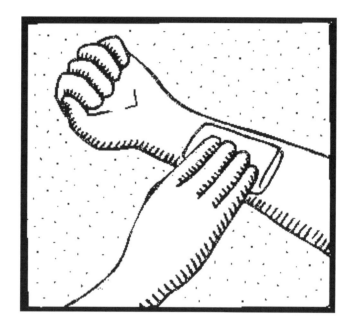

**How to Play:** Select several players to be the chasers and hand each one an identification vest or a foam ball for tagging.

On a starting signal, the chasers attempt to tag the other players. Once tagged, the injured player immediately grabs the spot where he/she was tagged and keeps playing. The tagger must then tag another player—no consecutive tags are allowed on one player. When tagged a second time, the injured player uses their other hand to apply pressure to that spot, and then continues to run. If the injured player is tagged a third time, they become an additional Tagger (and will need a foam ball or identification vest). The new Taggers immediately begin chasing others.

Play is continuous until all are Taggers.

# Fitness Tag

**Introduction:** This high-energy game increases muscular endurance and strength.

**Equipment:** One box of foam balls for the taggers (enough for most of the players)

**How to Play:** Before play, review three specific exercises that the players are to perform if tagged. This can include push-ups, crunches, squats, planks, jumping jacks, and so forth. Announce to the players the three exercises they are to complete if tagged.

Select several players to be the chasers and hand each a foam ball for tagging. Put the remainder of the foam balls in a box by the side of the play area. The rest of the players start scattered around the play area.

On a starting signal, the chasers attempt to tag the other players. The first time players are tagged, they have to do exercise #1 (for example, 10 jumping jacks) off to the side of the play area before returning again. The second time they are tagged, they have to do exercise #2 (for example, 10 push-ups). The third time they have to do exercise #3 (for example, 10 crunches). The fourth time requires the player to take a foam ball out of the box and become a tagger. No player can be tagged while performing an exercise.

Play stops when all players have become taggers.

# Flexibility Tag

**Introduction:** This tag game mixes various stretching exercises with healthy jogging.

**Equipment:** One box of foam balls for the taggers (enough for most of the players)

**How to Play:** Before play, review three stretching exercises that the players are to perform if tagged. This can include standing hamstring stretches, lower leg stretches, shoulder/arm stretches, and so forth. Announce to the players the three stretches, in order, that they are to perform during the game.

Select several players to be the chasers and hand each a foam ball for tagging. Put the remainder of the foam balls in a box by the side of the play area. The rest of the players start scattered around the play area.

On a starting signal, the chasers attempt to tag the other players. The first time players are tagged, they have to do stretch #1 (for example, 30 seconds stretching the hamstrings) off to the side of the play area before returning again. The second time they are tagged, they have to do stretch #2 (for example, 30 seconds stretching the lower legs). The third time they have to do stretch #3 (for example, 30 seconds stretching the shoulders and arms). The fourth time requires the player to take a foam ball out of the box and become a tagger. No player can be tagged while stretching.

Play stops when all players have become taggers.

# Football Tag

**Introduction:** This game builds cardiovascular endurance and allows children the opportunity to practice the skills of centering and catching a football.

**Equipment:** Several player identification vests for the "tacklers" (that is, the taggers), and several foam footballs for the "quarterbacks" (that is, the rescuers).

**How to Play:** Select several players to be the "tacklers," or taggers, and hand each one an identification vest for tagging. Also, select several players to be the "quarterbacks," or rescuers, and hand each a foam football.

Before play, it's important to review the proper form of hiking a football and catching a hiked ball.

On a starting signal, the chasers attempt to tag the other players. Once tagged, the player must freeze in a 3-point stance with one hand on the ground. A quarterback can free the frozen player by handing him/her the football, and both players perform a centering of the football. This is done by having the quarterback receiving a pass from the centering player (who is in a centering stance position) after he or she yells out "Ready, Set, Hike." After a successful execution of the centering of the football, the quarterback moves on to find someone else who needs to be rescued.

Play is continuous. Select new taggers and quarterbacks often.

# Frosty the Snowman Tag

**Introduction:** This game develops cardiovascular endurance and allows children to participate in an atmosphere of holiday fun.

**Equipment:**  Five foam balls for the taggers and rescuers

**How to Play:**  Select three players to be the "sunshine" chasers and two players to be the "snowmen" rescuers. Identify these players with different colored balls or identification vests (ideal colors would be white for the snow rescuers and yellow for the sunshine players).

On a starting signal, the sunshine chasers attempt to tag the other players. Once tagged, players become frozen in a "snowman" position and start slowly melting to the ground. The snowmen can be rescued from the melting process by one of the two rescue players. This is done by having the rescuer gently touch the melting snowman on the top of the head with the white fleece ball. No rescuing player can be tagged by a sunshine player.

Play is continuous. Select new chasers and rescuers often.

# Funny Face Tag

**Introduction:** This fun game brings a guaranteed element of humor to playing tag. It also calls for total participation by everyone.

**Equipment:** Several player identification vests or foam balls for the taggers

**How to Play:** Select several players to be the chasers and hand each one an identification vest or a foam ball for tagging.

On a starting signal, the chasers attempt to tag the other players. Once tagged, the player stands stationary with one hand held high. The tagged player can be freed once a free player stands directly in front of him/her and makes a funny face. No player can be tagged while making a funny face.

Play is continuous. Select new chasers often.

# Gator Tag

**Introduction:** This game requires a lot of cooperation and keeps everyone moving!

**Equipment:** Three or four long jump ropes (16' feet long)

**How to Play:** Select three or four players to start out as the "Gators" (taggers). Each Gator is also given a long rope to drag behind them with one hand.

On a starting signal, the Gators attempt to tag the other players with one hand while holding a rope with the other hand. Once tagged, players must hold on the rope with the Gator making the tag—and each subsequent tagged player also holds on to the rope. Only the Gator at the head of the rope can make tags. If the Gator breaks or must stop for any reason, then the players have to reconnect before resuming. The objective is to stay free of the growing Gators.

Play is continuous until all players are linked to a Gator.

# Geography Tag

**Introduction:** This game integrates the playing of tag with social studies—in this case, the learning of state capitols. It's also a great aerobic activity since play is continuous.

**Equipment:**  Several player identification vests or foam balls for the taggers

**How to Play:**  Before play, spend time identifying the names of state capitols.

Select several players to be the chasers and hand each one an identification vest or foam ball for tagging. The remaining players start scattered around the play area.

On a starting signal, the chasers attempt to tag the other players. Once tagged, the player must go down on one knee with one hand held high in the air while waiting for help. Tagged players can be set free when a free player gives them the name of a state and they correctly answer with the name of the capitol.  If incorrect, then the helping player is allowed to give "clues." A helping player cannot be tagged.

Play is continuous. Select new chasers often.

# Germ Tag

**Introduction:** Here is a fun total-participation game for use as an instant starter and/or as an activity in physical education to develop aerobic endurance.

**Equipment:** Foam balls for the taggers

**How to Play:** This game will require a higher than normal number of chasers—about one chaser for every five players is ideal. Select players to be the chasers and hand each one a foam ball (a "germ") for tagging.

On a starting signal, the chasers (players holding a "germ"—that is, a ball) attempt to tag the other players. Once tagged, the player takes the germ and immediately attempts to tag another player. No tag-backs are allowed—that is, a tagged player is not allowed to tag the player who just tagged him/her. The objective is to get rid of the germ as fast as possible, while avoiding being tagged by the other player with a germ.

Play is continuous until time is called.

# Good Manners Tag

**Introduction:** Here is a fun tag game reinforces the practice of good manners. It's also a great aerobic activity since play is continuous.

**Equipment:** Several player identification vests or foam balls for the taggers

**How to Play:** Select several players to be the chasers and hand each one an identification vest or foam ball for tagging.

On a starting signal, the chasers attempt to tag the other players. Once tagged, the player must go down on both knees with one hand held high in the air while waiting for help. Another player can free the tagged player by politely asking, "May I help you?" The tagged player must respond, "Yes, please." The helping player then extends a hand and helps the tagged player up on his/her feet. The tagged player then says, "Thank you," and the helper responds with, "You're welcome." Both players are now able to re-enter the game. A helping player cannot be tagged.

Play is continuous. Select new chasers often.

# Groundhog Day Tag

**Introduction:** Here is a game that develops cardiovascular endurance and is sure to be a child favorite around the annual Groundhogs Day.

**Equipment:** An equal number of different-colored foam balls for the two categories of taggers

**How to Play:** Select an equal number of two or three players to be the "Sunshine" chasers, and two to three players to be the "Storm" players. Identify these players with different colored balls or identification vests. All other players are groundhogs.

Before play, explain the background and history of Groundhog Day. If the groundhog sees its shadow, it means six more weeks of winter. Spring arrives soon if the groundhog sees clouds.

Designate a marked off corner area of the gym as the exercise "den." On a starting signal, both the Sunshine and Storm chasers attempt to tag the other players. Once tagged by a Storm chaser, players jump as high as possible and yell out "Spring is coming!" Afterwards, they are immediately free to resume play. However, if tagged by one the Sunshine players, they have seen their shadows and must now go to the exercise den to do an exercise of their choice for five counts (push-ups, jumping jacks, squats, etc.)—afterwards, they are free to resume play.

Play is continuous. Select new chasers often.

# High Five Tag

**Introduction:** This easy-to-understand game is an excellent instant starter to get children energized at the beginning of a physical education class or play period.

**Equipment:** Foam balls for the taggers

**How to Play:** This game will require a higher than normal number of chasers—about one chaser for every five to eight players is ideal. Select players to be the chasers and hand each one a foam ball for tagging.

On a starting signal, the chasers attempt to tag the other players. Once tagged, players stand in a stationary position with one hand held high, palms showing. Tagged players can be freed if a free player "high fives" their palm. The objective is to last as long as possible without being tagged.

Play is continuous until time is called.

# Hula Hoop Tag

**Introduction:** Here is a game that combines lots of movement, callisthenic exercises, and fun!

**Equipment:** One hula hoop for each player

**How to Play:** All players start with a hula hoop. If possible, try to equalize the number of same-colored hoops handed out (that is, the same number of red, blue, yellow, etc., hoops).

Before play, have players independently practice rolling their hoops. Challenge them to roll for increasingly greater distances and in different directions. Once this skill is mastered, they are ready for play.

Designate a specific color of hula hoop to start out as the taggers. Also, specify a particular exercise for tagged players. For example, players with a blue hoop can be designated as the game's first taggers; and, players who have their hoops touched by a blue hoop are to perform six push-ups before becoming free again. Other exercise choices could be performing jumping jacks, crunches, jogging-in-place, etc.

On a starting signal, all players start out by rolling their hoops around the play area—with the players chosen as the taggers also rolling their hoops and attempting to tag others by touching their hoops. Once tagged, a player must perform the required exercise to become free again.

Play is continuous. Select players with a different-colored hoop to become new taggers throughout the game, and select new exercises with each change of color.

# I Love PE! Tag

**Introduction:** This high-energy game provides a fun way for children to express their love for physical education!

**Equipment:** Several player identification vests or foam balls for the taggers

**How to Play:** Select several players to be the chasers and hand each one an identification vest or a foam ball for tagging.

On a starting signal, the chasers attempt to tag the other players. Once tagged, the player immediately goes to the middle of the gym, jumps as high as possible, and yells out "I love PE!" The tagged player is then free to exit the circle and move about. No player can be tagged while jumping in the middle circle and yelling.

Play is continuous. Select new chasers often.

# Invisible Basketball Tag

**Introduction:** This game builds cardiovascular endurance and allows children the opportunity to practice the basketball "jump shot" and "lay-up" at the same time.

**Equipment:** Several player identification vests or foam balls for the taggers

**How to Play:** Select several players to be the chasers and hand each one an identification vest or a foam ball for tagging.

Before play, it's important to review the proper form of executing a jump shot and the lay-up shot used in basketball.

On a starting signal, the chasers attempt to tag the other players. Once tagged, the player must freeze with both arms held high. Another player can free the frozen player by standing directly in front of him/her and pretending to shoot a basketball (using the jump shot form) over the frozen player's outstretched arms. Alternatively, the frozen player and rescuer can choose to perform an imaginary lay-up together. This is done by having both players use the hand and knee on the same side of their bodies, and going up at the same time to high-five the hands.

Play is continuous. Select new chasers often.

# Invisible Jump Rope Tag

**Introduction:** This unique game allows players to practice various jump rope techniques (without the rope) while playing tag. It also enhances cardiovascular health.

**Equipment:** Three or more player identification vests or foam balls for the taggers

**How to Play:** Before play, review the proper technique of performing various jump rope skills such as the two-foot, skier, bell, straddle, and so forth. Have the children practice these skills with "invisible" ropes.

Depending on the size of the group, select three or more players to be the taggers, and hand each one an identification vest or a foam ball for tagging. Players spread out in the play area.

On a starting signal, the taggers move around and attempt to tag the others. Once tagged, players must stop and do 10 jumps with their "invisible" rope. After finishing their jumps, they stand with one hand held high in the air. Once a free player gives them a "high-five," they are free to rejoin the game.

A variation of above is to have players become taggers once caught (instead of jumping rope) so that the taggers are always changing—and, free players can avoid getting tagged by performing invisible jump rope skills once a tagger gets near them.

Play is continuous.

# Isometric Crab Tag

**Introduction:** This is an excellent tag game for introducing an "isometric" exercise position. An isometric exercise is done in a static position during which the joint angle and muscle length do not change during contraction. In this case, the static hold position is a "crab" position.

**Equipment:** Several player identification vests or foam balls for the taggers; several beanbags for the rescuers

**How to Play:** Before play, review the proper execution of the "crab" position. This is having hands and feet on the floor while facing upward (that is, an "upside down push-up" type of position). Also explain the difference between an isometric and isotonic (full range of movement) exercise.

Select several players to be the "Taggers," and hand each one an identification vest or a foam ball for tagging. Also select several players to begin as "Rescuers," and hand each a beanbag.

On a starting signal, the taggers attempt to tag the other players. Once tagged, players freeze in the "crab" position. They have to hold this position until a rescuer comes by, helps them up, and gives them a beanbag. The beanbag now belongs to the player who was holding the crab position and now he/she becomes a rescuer. The former rescuer now becomes a regular free player. Rescuers can never be tagged.

Play is continuous. Select new chasers often.

# Juggle Tag

**Introduction:** This high-energy game provides an opportunity for children to practice juggling skills while getting a lot of healthy movement.

**Equipment:** Several player identification vests or foam balls for the taggers and several boxes of juggling scarves or balls (enough for at least half of the players).

**How to Play:** Before play, review various juggling routines with the scarves, beanbags, and juggling balls. For beginning jugglers, use a simple cross-body toss and catch first. Use two or three juggling items for older or more advanced players.

Select several players to be the chasers and hand each one an identification vest or a foam ball for tagging. Place several boxes of juggling scarves, beanbags, or juggling balls around the outside of the play area—using the boundary lines of an inside basketball court is ideal.

On a starting signal, the chasers attempt to tag the other players. Once tagged, the player immediately goes to the nearest box of juggling equipment and attempts at least three juggling movements. The tagged player then puts the equipment back into the box and is now free to move about again. No player can be tagged while juggling.

Play is continuous. Select new chasers often.

# Jumping Jack Tag

**Introduction:** This game injects the jumping jack exercise with the game of tag, and increases cardiovascular health.

**Equipment:** Three or more player identification vests or foam balls for the taggers

**How to Play:** Before play, review the proper technique of performing a jumping jack exercise.

Depending on the size of the group, select three or more players to be the taggers, and hand each one an identification vest or a foam ball for tagging. Players spread out in the play area.

On a starting signal, the taggers move around and attempt to tag the others. Once tagged, players must stop and do 10 jumping jacks (younger children can perform less). After finishing the jumping jacks, they stand with one hand held high in the air. Once a free player gives them a "high-five," they are free to rejoin the game.

Play is continuous.

# Leapfrog Tag

**Introduction:** This active game incorporates the skill of jumping with lots of movement. For safety purposes, it is important the correct leapfrog form be taught prior to playing the game.

**Equipment:** Several player identification vests or foam balls for the taggers

**How to Play:** Select several players to be the chasers and hand each one an identification vest or a foam ball for tagging.

On a starting signal, the chasers attempt to tag the other players. Once tagged, the player freezes in the "frog" position (that is, squatting low with both hands on the floor for stability, and head tucked). The frog can be freed by having a player leapfrog over him/her. No player can be tagged while leapfrogging.

Play is continuous. Select new chasers often.

# Line Tag

**Introduction:** Here is a simple and easy-to-understand tag game that utilizes the lines of a basketball court (either indoors or outdoors) and builds cardiovascular endurance.

**Equipment:** Several foam balls for the taggers

**How to Play:** Select several players to be the taggers and hand each a foam ball for tagging. Have all players (including the beginning taggers) start by standing on a line anywhere around the basketball court.

On a starting signal, the chasers attempt to tag the other players—all players and taggers have to stay on the lines while chasing and fleeing. Additionally, taggers are not allowed to throw the ball. Once tagged, a player takes the ball and becomes a new tagger. Thus, there are new taggers throughout the game. The objective for all players is to be a tagger as few times as possible.

Play is continuous.

# Loose Caboose Tag

**Introduction:** This fun game builds cardiovascular activity and requires no equipment.

**Equipment:** None

**How to Play:** Choose 3 or 4 players to start as the "Its." These "Its" represent the "loose cabooses" because they aren't connected to a train. Organize the other players into groups of three or four, and have each group form a "train" by holding onto the hips or shoulders of the player in front of them. Trains must stay joined together as they move about the play area.

On a starting signal, the "trains" are free to move around the play area. Meanwhile, the "Its" try to attach themselves to the end of a train. When the loose cabooses attach themselves, they yell out "loose caboose," and the front player in the train now leaves the train and becomes a loose caboose. Play continues in this fashion until time is called.

For fair play, do not allow loose cabooses to tag the same train that he or she was just a part of.

# Math Tag

**Introduction:** This is an active tag game that integrates math concepts with movement.

**Equipment:** Several foam balls or identification vests for the taggers

**How to Play:** Before play, review the math concepts that will be used. This can be in the areas of addition, multiplication, division, and so forth.

Select several players to be the chasers and hand each one a foam ball (or wear an identification vest) for tagging.

On a starting signal, the chasers attempt to tag the other players. Once tagged, the player immediately freezes with one hand held high. A free player can rescue a tagged player by standing directly in front of him/her and calling out a math question (for example, what is 10 + 10?) to be answered. Tagged players who answer the math questions correctly are back in the game. If an answer is incorrect, the rescuing free player can give "clues" until the correct answer is given, or the tagged player can wait for a different player to come by with another math question.

Play is continuous until time is called.

# Mirror Tag

**Introduction:** This is a fun and high-energy tag game that is appropriate for children in all elementary grades. It's also a nice creative activity since play requires an expression of unique balances and body shapes.

**Equipment:** Several player identification vests or foam balls for the taggers

**How to Play:** Select several players to be the chasers and hand each one an identification vest or a foam ball for tagging.

On a starting signal, the chasers attempt to tag the other players. Once tagged, the player must freeze and form a unique balance position or body shape. Another player can free the frozen player by standing directly in front of him/her and form the exact balance or body shape for five seconds. Players can count out loud together for the five second hold. When done, both players high five and now the frozen player is freed.

Play is continuous. Select new chasers often.

# Muscle Tag

**Introduction:** Here is a fitness-building game that also reinforces the anatomical names of muscles.

**Equipment:** Several foam balls or identification vests for the taggers

**How to Play:** Before play, review the names of various muscles around the body and their location (for example, the biceps, triceps, quadriceps, and so forth).

Select several players to be the chasers and hand each one a foam ball (or wear an identification vest) for tagging.

On a starting signal, the chasers attempt to tag the other players. Once tagged, the player immediately freezes with a finger on a specific muscle. A free player can rescue a tagged player by standing directly in front of him/her and successfully identify the name of the muscle. If the guess is incorrect, the tagged player can then give "clues" until the correct answer is given, or he or she can wait for another player to come by with the correct answer.

An alternative to "Muscle Tag" is to play "Bone Tag." The game would be played exactly as explained above, but now the challenge is to name the correct bones of the body. This could be the tibia, fibula, femur, scapula, etc.

Play is continuous until time is called.

# North Wind-South Wind

**Introduction:** This fun and easy-to-understand game develops cardiovascular endurance.

**Equipment:** Several player identification vests or foam balls for the taggers

**How to Play:** Select three players to be the "North Wind" chasers and two players to be the "South Wind" players. Identify these players with different colored balls or identification vests. Before play, explain the concept of the "freezing" north wind, and the "unfreezing" effect of the wind that comes from the south.

On a starting signal, the North Wind chasers attempt to tag the other players. Once tagged, players become frozen and stands with legs together and both arms stretched upward. The frozen players can be unfrozen by one of the two South Wind players. No South Wind player can be tagged by a North Wind player.

Play is continuous. Select new chasers often.

# Oger Tag

**Introduction:** This imaginative game is patterned after the movie Shrek. It develops cardiovascular endurance and muscular strength.

**Equipment:** Four foam balls or vests for the taggers; four foam balls or vests of a different color for the rescuers

**How to Play:** Select four players to be the chasers (Fairy Godmother, Lord Farquaad, Prince Charming, and Rumpelstilskin) and four players to be the rescuers (Shrek, Princess Fiona, Puss-in-Boots, and Donkey). Identify these players with different colored balls or identification vests.

On a starting signal, the evil chasers (the four players designated as the Fairy Godmother, Lord Farquaad, Prince Charming, and Rumpelstilskin) attempt to tag the other players. Players who are tagged must perform, in place, one of four different exercise choices—jumping jacks, planks, push-ups, or mountain climbers). Meanwhile, the rescuers (the four players designated as Shrek, Donkey, Puss-in-Boots, and Princess Fiona) move around and rescue the exercising players by gently touching them on the shoulders. Shrek, Princess Fiona, Donkey, and Puss-in-Boots can never be tagged by a chaser.

Play is continuous.

# Push-Up Tag

**Introduction:** This is an excellent tag game for developing core strength and cardiovascular health.

**Equipment:** Several player identification vests or foam balls for the taggers; several beanbags for the rescuers

**How to Play:** Before play, review the proper execution of the push-up plank hold.

Select several players to be the "Taggers," and hand each one an identification vest or a foam ball for tagging. Also select several players to begin as "Rescuers," and hand each a beanbag.

On a starting signal, the taggers attempt to tag the other players. Once tagged, players freeze in the "up" position of a push-up or plank hold. They have to hold this position until a rescuer comes by and places a beanbag on their back. The beanbag now belongs to the player who was holding the push-up/plank position and now he/she becomes a rescuer. The former rescuer now becomes a regular free player. Rescuers can never be tagged.

Play is continuous. Select new chasers often.

# Quadriceps Tag

**Introduction:** This is an excellent tag game for developing leg strength (especially in the quadriceps and gluteal muscles) as well as enhancing cardiovascular endurance.

**Equipment:** Several player identification vests or foam balls for the taggers, and several beanbags for the rescuers.

**How to Play:** Before play, review the proper technique used in the wall sit exercise.

Select several players to be the "Taggers," and hand each one an identification vest or a foam ball for tagging. Also select several players to begin as "Rescuers," and hand each a beanbag.

On a starting signal, the taggers attempt to tag the other players. Once tagged, players go to a surrounding wall and assume a wall sit position. The wall sit is done by facing away from the wall (about a foot away), leaning the back against the wall, and assuming a squat position with knees flexed at a 90-degree angle. They have to hold this position until a rescuer comes by and places a beanbag in their hands. The beanbag now belongs to the player who was holding the wall sit position and now he/she becomes a rescuer. The former rescuer now becomes a regular free player. Rescuers can never be tagged.

Play is continuous. Select new chasers often.

# Rock, Paper, Scissors Tag

**Introduction:** This exciting game is a great choice as an instant starter and/or for use as an icebreaker in a physical education class or recreational setting.

**Equipment:** None

**How to Play:** This game combines the excitement of playing rock-paper-scissors with the fun of playing tag. Before play, review the rules of playing rock-paper-scissors (see the diagram below). Every player begins by spreading out anywhere around the play area in a stationary position.

On a starting signal, each player spins around once (in one spot) and attempts to tag the closest player. Once tagged, the two players immediately play a "best-out-of-one" game of rock-paper-scissors. After finishing, both players spin around once in on one spot and gives chase to another player. Play continues in this fashion until time is called. The objective is to win as many games of rock-paper-scissors as possible.

As a safety consideration, do not allow players to run. Also, remind players to be considerate of others as they move around.

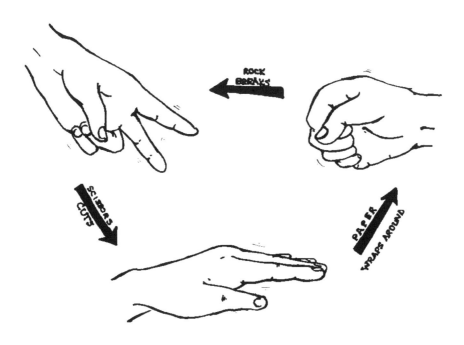

# Sign Language Tag

**Introduction:** Here is a great total-participation game that allows children to practice the hand gestures related to sign language, while at the same time, engaged in a lot of healthy movement.

**Equipment:** Foam balls or identification vests for the taggers

**How to Play:** Before play, review the sign language letters that the players have previously learned.

Select players to be the chasers and hand each one a foam ball (or wear an identification vest) for tagging.

On a starting signal, the chasers attempt to tag the other players. Once tagged, the player immediately freezes and makes a sign language letter. A free player can rescue a tagged player by standing directly in front of him/her, and successfully naming the correct letter. If the guess is incorrect, the tagged player can then give "clues" until the correct answer is given. Players cannot be tagged while rescuing others.

Play is continuous until time is called.

# Skunk Tag

**Introduction:** This fitness-building game brings a guaranteed element of humor and fun to playing tag.

**Equipment:** Several player identification vests or foam balls for the taggers

**How to Play:** Select several players to be the chasers and hand each one an identification vest or a foam ball for tagging.

On a starting signal, the chasers attempt to tag the other players. Once tagged, players assume a stationary stance with one arm under a knee and fingers on the nose. An alternative frozen stance would be grab one foot and bring it to the nose. For children unable to perform either frozen stance, another option would be to jump up and down on one foot with the nose held. The tagged player can be freed once a free player lightly touches him/her on the shoulder.

Play is continuous. Select new chasers often.

# Spelling Tag

**Introduction:** This active tag game integrates healthy movement with the spelling concepts commonly used in physical education.

**Equipment:** Several foam balls or identification vests for the taggers

**How to Play:** Before play, review the "spelling list" that will be used. Try to list words that are commonly used in a PE class. This can be going over the correct spelling and meaning of words (such as, exercise, fitness, aerobic, jogging, heart, pulse, game, jumping, dance, ball, sports, tag, walking, and so forth).

Select several players to be the chasers and hand each one a foam ball (or wear an identification vest) for tagging.

On a starting signal, the chasers attempt to tag the other players. Once tagged, the player immediately freezes with one hand held high. Free players can rescue tagged players by standing directly in front of them and calling out a word from the "spelling list" to be spelled (for example, how do you spell "muscle?"). Tagged players who answer the spelling questions correctly are back in the game. If an answer is incorrect, the rescuing free player can give "clues" until the correct answer is given, or the tagged player can wait for a different player to come by with another spelling question.

Play is continuous until time is called.

# Sports Tag

**Introduction:** Here is an aerobic tag game that allows children to show others what their favorite sport activities are.

**Equipment:** Foam balls or identification vests for the taggers

**How to Play:** Select players to be the chasers and hand each one a foam ball (or wear an identification vest) for tagging.

On a starting signal, the chasers attempt to tag the other players. Once tagged, the player immediately freezes into a sport statue (that is, a baseball player in a batting position, a basketball player in a shooting position, a soccer player kicking, etc.). A free player can rescue a tagged player by standing directly in front of him/her, and successfully guessing the name of the sport. If the guess is incorrect, the tagged player can then give "clues" until the correct answer is given.

Play is continuous until time is called.

# Statue of Liberty Tag

**Introduction:** This patriotic-theme game provides plenty of healthy movement and fun.

**Equipment:** Foam balls or identification vests for the taggers

**How to Play:** Select several players to be the chasers and hand each one a foam ball (or wear an identification vest) for tagging.

On a starting signal, the chasers attempt to tag the other players. Once tagged, the player immediately freezes in a motionless position depicting the Statue of Liberty (that is, standing with one arm held high and upward). A free player can rescue a statue player by standing directly in front of him/her, together they repeat the words "Go USA!" and then high-five each other. No free player can be tagged while trying to rescue a statue player.

Play is continuous until time is called.

# Stinger Tag

**Introduction:** This high-energy "team" game requires a lot of chasing, fleeing, dodging, and tagging.

**Equipment:** One foam ball for each player; distribute an equal number of four different colors.

**How to Play:** Divide the players into four equal teams, and give each team a colored ball (Team #1 has blue; Team #2 has red, and so forth). Players spread out in the play area.

Designate a specific color to start out as the taggers (called the "stingers"). On a starting signal, the team players with that color chase and tag the players with different colors. Once tagged, a player stands stationary with the ball held high. A player of any colored ball (other than the tagging team) can free the frozen player by "high-fiving" him or her. The objective for the tagging team is to freeze everyone on the other teams to end the game.

Play is continuous. Select a new color after a minute or two so that each team has a chance to be "stingers."

# Stone Age Tag

**Introduction:** This imaginative and fun game develops cardiovascular fitness.

**Equipment:** Two or three foam balls for the "barbarians" (or taggers); two or three foam bowling pins for the "cavemen" (or rescuers).

**How to Play:** Select two or three players to be the "Barbarians" (or taggers), and two or three players to be the "Cavemen" (or rescuers). Identify these players with foam balls for the Barbarians and foam bowling pins (called the "clubs") for the Cavemen.

On a starting signal, the Barbarians chase and attempt to tag the other players with the foam balls (no throwing is allowed). Players who are tagged stay in a frozen position with one hand held high. Meanwhile, the Cavemen can unfreeze the tagged players by handing them his/her club. Therefore, the rescuers or Cavemen are continuously switching off throughout the game. A rescuer or Caveman can never be tagged by a Barbarian.

Play is continuous.

# Stoplight Tag

**Introduction:** This endurance-building game is perfect for children in the primary grades.

**Equipment:** Several red-colored player identification vests or foam balls for the taggers (the "Stop" players); several green-colored identification vests or foam balls for the rescuers (the "Go" players)

**How to Play:** Select three players to be the "Stop" players (or chasers), and three players to be the "Go" players (or rescuers). Identify these players with red colored balls or identification vests for the chasers, and green colored vests or balls for the rescuers. Before play, explain the concept of a "stoplight" —with red meaning "stop," and green meaning to "go."

On a starting signal, the "Stop" players (that is, the chasers) attempt to tag the other players. Once tagged, players become frozen and stand with legs together and both arms stretched upward. The frozen players can only be unfrozen by one of the three "Go" players (that is, the rescuers)—and this is done by having both the frozen player and the "Go" player giving each other a 'high-five." No "Go" player can be tagged by a "Stop" player.

Play is continuous. Select new chasers often.

# Stork Tag

**Introduction:** This maximum participation game has lots of movement, balance, and fun!

**Equipment:** Several player identification vests or foam balls for the taggers

**How to Play:** Select several players to be the chasers and hand each one an identification vest or a foam ball for tagging.

On a starting signal, the chasers attempt to tag the other players. Once tagged, the players assume a one-legged stork stance with one knee held high (foot not touching the floor) and arms held to side as "wings." The tagged player can be freed once a free player gently touches his/her knee (the knee held in the air).

Play is continuous. Select new chasers often.

# Stuck in the Mud

**Introduction:** Here is a fun tag game that is a nice aerobic activity since play is continuous.

**Equipment:** Several player identification vests or foam balls for the taggers

**How to Play:** Select several players to be the chasers and hand each one an identification vest or foam ball for tagging.

On a starting signal, the chasers attempt to tag the other players. Once tagged, the player must go down on both knees with one hand held high in the air—he or she is stuck in the mud. Another player can free the stuck player by grabbing their hand and pulling them upward out of the mud.

Play is continuous. Select new chasers often.

# Sun Tag

**Introduction:** Here is a simple and easy-to-understand game for use as an instant starter, warm-up activity, and/or to develop cardiovascular endurance in a physical education class.

**Equipment:** Several player identification vests or foam balls for the taggers

**How to Play:** Select several players to be the chasers and hand each one an identification vest or foam ball for tagging.

On a starting signal, the chasers attempt to tag the other players. Once tagged, the player becomes an "icicle" and stands with legs wide apart and arms stretched upright (as in the open part of the jumping jack exercise). The icicle can be unfrozen by a "sun," that is, any unfrozen player who crawls through an icicle's legs. No sun can be tagged while crawling through an icicle's legs.

Play is continuous. Select new chasers often.

# Swim Tag

**Introduction:** This tag game is derived from the movie Nemo, and combines swimming arm movements with jogging.

**Equipment:** Several player identification vests or foam balls for the "Barracudas" (taggers); several vests or foam balls of a different color for the "Nemos" (rescuers)

**How to Play:** Select several players to be the "Barracudas" (taggers), and hand each one an identification vest or a foam ball for tagging. Also choose several players to be the "Nemos" (rescuers), and hand each one a different colored vest or foam ball.

Before play, introduce the arm patterns of several swim strokes. For example, the breaststroke, crawl, and backstroke can all be performed in a standing position (and slightly bent over).

On a starting signal, the "Barracudas" attempt to tag the other players. Once tagged, the players stand in a stationary position and perform arm movements as if swimming—this can mimic the breaststroke, crawl, or backstroke. The swimmer can be freed once a "Nemo" rescuer gently touches his/her shoulder. "Nemos" cannot be tagged by a "Barracuda" player.

Play is continuous. Select new chasers often.

# Teamwork Tag

**Introduction:** This active tag game incorporates the skills of cooperation and teamwork.

**Equipment:** Several player identification vests or foam balls for the taggers

**How to Play:** Select several players to be the chasers and hand each one an identification vest or a foam ball for tagging.

Before play, explain the concept of working with others to accomplish a goal or task. On a starting signal, the chasers attempt to tag the other players. Once tagged, the player freezes in a stationary position with both arms held high. The frozen player can be freed when two free players place their right hands on top of the frozen player's right hand and all three players yell out "teamwork works!" together. Free players cannot be tagged while rescuing others.

Play is continuous. Select new chasers often.

# Thankful Tag

**Introduction:** Here is a game that works great as either a warm-up activity or as an ending activity in physical education. It also sets a positive tone for children as everyone enjoys being appreciated.

**Equipment:** Several foam balls or identification vests for the taggers

**How to Play:** Before play, review the concept of being thankful for someone and how to express thankfulness.

Select several players to be the chasers and hand each one a foam ball (or wear an identification vest) for tagging.

On a starting signal, the chasers attempt to tag the other players. Once tagged, players immediately freeze in a standing position with one hand held high. A free player can unfreeze a frozen player by telling him/her what they are specifically thankful for. An example would be saying "thank you for being my friend," or "thank you for sitting with me at lunch." Both players then "high five" each other and rejoin the game.

Play is continuous until time is called. Choose new taggers periodically.

# Tire Tag

**Introduction:** This game is a great cardiovascular workout since the game is practically non-stop for both the chasers and "cars."

**Equipment:** Several player identification vests or foam balls for the taggers

**How to Play:** Select several players to be the chasers and hand each one an identification vest or foam ball for tagging.

On a starting signal, the chasers attempt to tag the other players (the "cars"). Once tagged, the car gets a flat tire and must go down on all fours with one elbow collapsed on the floor. Another player can fix the flat tire and free the broken down car by lightly touching its shoulder or head and saying "honk, honk." The car now has its flat tire fixed and is free to drive away.

Play is continuous. Select new chasers periodically.

# Toad Tag

**Introduction:** This fun game combines the movement of jumping (as a frog) along with a lot of jogging or other locomotor patterns. For instructional purposes, it is important that the correct frog jumping form be taught prior to playing the game.

**Equipment:** Several player identification vests or foam balls for the taggers

**How to Play:** Select several players to be the chasers and hand each one an identification vest or a foam ball for tagging.

On a starting signal, the chasers attempt to tag the other players. Once tagged, the player immediately gets into a "frog" position (that is, squatting low with both hands on the floor), and begins jumping around like a frog. The frog can be freed by having a free player lightly touch him/her on the shoulder.

Play is continuous. Select new chasers often.

# Tornado Tag

**Introduction:** This aerobic game incorporates the skill of cooperation.

**Equipment:** Several player identification vests or foam balls for the taggers

**How to Play:** Select several players to be the chasers and hand each one an identification vest or a foam ball for tagging.

On a starting signal, the chasers attempt to tag the other players. Once tagged, the player freezes in a stationary position with both arms held high. The frozen player can be freed when two free players hold hands in a circle around the frozen player and circle twice (thus, the "tornado" action). Free players cannot be tagged while performing the tornado twist.

Play is continuous. Select new chasers often.

# Toy Story Tag

**Introduction:** This fun and imaginative game develops cardiovascular endurance.

**Equipment:** Two foam balls or vests for the taggers; and two foam balls or vests of a different color for the rescuers.

**How to Play:** Select two players to be the chasers (named "Zurg" and "Sid") and two players to be the rescuers ("Woody" and "Buzz"). Identify these players with different colored balls or identification vests.

On a starting signal, Zurg and Sid chase and attempt to tag the other players. Players who are tagged must get down in a stationary squatting position. Meanwhile, Woody and Buzz move around and rescue the frozen players by gently touching them on the shoulders. Woody and Buzz can never be tagged by Zurg and Sid.

Play is continuous.

# Tunnel Tag

**Introduction:** This activity, sometimes called "Frozen Tag," is a classic and is probably the most played tag game by children around the world. Its name is derived from the position that tagged players must hold once they are caught and waiting to be freed.

**Equipment:** Several player identification vests or foam balls for the taggers

**How to Play:** Select several players to be the chasers and hand each one an identification vest or foam ball for tagging.

On a starting signal, the chasers attempt to tag the other players. Once tagged, the player forms a "tunnel" by standing with legs wide apart and arms by the sides. The tunnel player can be freed any unfrozen player who crawls through his/her legs from the back (for safety reasons, no player is allowed to go through the tunnel from an opposite direction). Also, no rescuing player can be tagged while crawling through a tunnel's legs.

Play is continuous. Select new chasers often.

# Turtle Tag

**Introduction:** Turtle Tag mainly develops cardiovascular endurance. Its name is derived from the position that tagged players must hold once caught and waiting to be freed.

**Equipment:** Several player identification vests or foam balls for the taggers

**How to Play:** Select several players to be the chasers and hand each one an identification vest or foam ball for tagging.

On a starting signal, the chasers attempt to tag the other players. Once tagged, the player forms an "upside turtle" by laying on his/her back with feet and arms up in the air wiggling around. A tagged turtle can be freed by any unfrozen player who gently pushes down on his/her foot or hand. Also, no rescuing player can be tagged while freeing a turtle.

Play is continuous. Select new chasers often.

# Virus Tag

**Introduction:** This imaginative game enhances aerobic fitness and introduces children to the health consequences of getting a "virus."

**Equipment:** Several foam balls for the "Virus" Taggers, and several pool noodles for the "Doctor" Rescuers.

**How to Play:** Before play, explain what a virus is and the consequences of a viral infection on someone's health.

Select several players to be the "Virus" taggers, and hand each one a foam ball for tagging. Also select several players to begin as "Doctor" rescuers, and hand each a pool noodle. The noodle represents a body temperature measurement device.

On a starting signal, the "Virus" taggers attempt to tag the other players. Once tagged, players go down onto their backs with their arms and legs sticking straight up. They can shake their arms and legs but they have to stay on their backs until a "Doctor" rescuer comes by, taps them lightly on the shoulder with the noodle, and says "No fever!" The tagged player is now "healthy" and free to move about. "Doctor" rescuers can never be tagged.

Play is continuous. Select new "Virus" taggers and "Doctor" rescuers often.

# Walk Tag

**Introduction:** This partner game is a great choice as an instant starter in physical education and/or for use in a limited play area.

**Equipment:** None

**How to Play:** Mark off a smaller than usual play area—this is because the players will be walking and will be tightly bunched together before play begins.

Have each player paired up with another. One of the players is designated as the chaser (a quick game of rock-paper-scissors is ideal for selecting the initial chaser). All pairs are initially standing together within a smaller than usual play area.

On a starting signal, each chaser spins around twice in one spot to give his/her partner an opportunity to flee. The chasers then attempt to tag their partner (walking only!). Once tagged, the partner immediately spins around twice on one spot and gives chase. Play continues in this fashion until time is called.

As a safety consideration, do not allow players to run. Also, remind players to be considerate of others as they move around in tight quarters.

# Wall Tunnel Tag

**Introduction:** This game is played somewhat like "Tunnel Tag" (see page 86). However, now tagged players must hold a half-handstand against a wall while waiting to be freed. It's a terrific activity for increasing upper-body strength and cardiovascular endurance.

**Equipment:** Several player identification vests or foam balls for the taggers

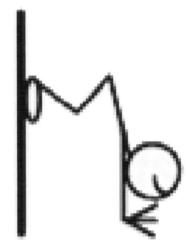

**How to Play:** Before play, review the "half-handstand" position against the wall and provide practice time.

Select several players to be the chasers and hand each one an identification vest or foam ball for tagging.

On a starting signal, the chasers attempt to tag the other players. Once tagged, players form a "tunnel" with their palms on the floor (about a foot from the wall), and slowly walk their feet up the wall. Their body should form a half-handstand against the wall as shown in the illustration above. The tunnel player can be freed any by any unfrozen player who crawls through his/her legs. No rescuing player can be tagged while crawling through a tunnel's legs.

Play is continuous. Select new chasers often.

# Wellness Tag

**Introduction:** This is an excellent tag game for developing cardiovascular health while enhancing the principles of a healthy lifestyle.

**Equipment:** Several foam balls for the "Unhealthy" taggers; several foam balls of a different color for the "Healthy" rescuers.

**How to Play:** Before play, explain how everyday choices affect their health and wellness. Discuss both healthy and unhealthy choices and list specific actions a person can take to increase overall wellness. Examples of healthy resolutions could be to exercise daily, eat more vegetables, get adequate sleep, etc.

Select several players to be the "Unhealthy" taggers, and hand each one a foam ball for tagging. Also select several players to begin as "Healthy" rescuers, and hand each a foam ball of a different color than the taggers.

On a starting signal, the "Unhealthy" taggers attempt to tag the other players. Once tagged, players freeze in a standing position with one hand held high. They have to hold this position until a "Healthy" rescuer comes by and ask for their new healthy choice resolution. The tagged player responds with a healthy choice resolution such as, "I'll start exercising daily," or "I'm going to eat less fried foods." After exchanging a "high-five," the tagged player is now free to move about. "Healthy" rescuers can never be tagged.

Play is continuous. Select new "Unhealthy" taggers and "Healthy" rescuers often.

# Workout Buddy Tag

**Introduction:** This active game increases cardiovascular endurance and muscular strength. It's always fun to exercise with a partner!

**Equipment:** One box of foam balls for the taggers (enough for most of the players)

**How to Play:** Before play, review three specific exercises that the players are to perform if tagged. This can include push-ups, crunches, squats, planks, jumping jacks, and so forth. Announce to the players the three exercises they are to complete if tagged.

Have all the of players partner up with each other and lock inside arms or hold hands. Select several pairs to be the chasers and hand each a foam ball for tagging. Put the remainder of the foam balls in a box by the side of the play area. The remaining pairs start scattered around the play area. Remind players that they have to stay joined with their partner throughout the game.

On a starting signal, the three pair of players who are the taggers move around and attempt to touch the other players with the ball. The first time a free pair is tagged, they have to do exercise #1 (for example, 10 jumping jacks) together off to the side of the play area before returning again. The second time they are tagged, they have to exercise #2 together (for example, 10 push-ups). The third time they have to do exercise #3 together (for example, 10 crunches). The fourth time requires the pair to take a foam ball out of the box and become taggers. No pair can be tagged while performing an exercise.

Play stops when all pairs have become taggers.

# Zoo Tag

**Introduction:** This tag game combines lots of healthy movement, imagination, and fun.

**Equipment:** Several player identification vests or foam balls for the taggers

**How to Play:** Select several players to be the "Zoo Animals" (the taggers) and hand each one an identification vest or a foam ball for tagging. The taggers announce which zoo animal they will represent—it can be any animal such as a lion, tiger, bear, elephant, and so forth

On a starting signal, the Zoo Animals attempt to tag the other players. Once tagged, the player immediately gets in a position that resembles the specific zoo animal that just tagged him/her and begins to move around the play area like that animal. The tagged animal player can be freed once a free player "high-fives" him/her.

Play is continuous. Select new Zoo Animals often.

# Zorro Tag

**Introduction:** This fun and imaginative game develops cardiovascular endurance.

**Equipment:** Five foam noodles

**How to Play:** Select three players to be the "Zorro's" (that is, the chasers) and two players to be the "Rescuers." Identify these players with different colored noodles (for example, the Zorro's could have red-colored noodles and the Rescuers could have blue-colored noodles).

On a starting signal, Zorro's take chase and attempt to tag the other players by touching them gently on the back with the noodle. Once tagged, players become frozen in a stationary position with the arms crossed in front of their chest (forming a "shield"). The shield indicates that they can no longer be tagged and need to be rescued. The tagged players can be freed by one of the two rescue players—and this is done by having the rescuer gently touch them on the back with their noodle. No Rescuer can be tagged by a Zorro.

Play is continuous. Select new chasers and rescuers often.

# Partner Beanbag Tag

**Introduction:** Using a partner's feet for a target, the players attempt to slide a beanbag and "tag" their shoes. This is great energizer that calls for maximum participation. For a large group, have all players find a partner and play multiple games simultaneously.

**Equipment:** One beanbag for each player

**How to Play:** The players start by facing each other with a beanbag in hand. Explain that both players need to stay within a few feet of each other throughout the game.

Using underhanded throws with the beanbags, the players attempt to tag either foot of the opponent while, at the same time, trying to keep their own feet from being tagged. Players can use a variety of circling and feinting movements before going for a quick underhanded throw to the foot. Touching the foot with an underhand slide of the beanbag is the only type of touch allowed—no overhand throwing is allowed. Each successful tag counts as one point. The objective is to end with the highest number of points.

# Partner Dice Tag

**Introduction:** This partner activity reinforces math skills and contains the chasing and fleeing element of tag. For a large group, have all players find a partner and play multiple games simultaneously using a center line and two safety lines.

**Equipment:** A pair of dice for each pair of players, ones for marking safety lines; and one poly spot for each pair of players.

**How to Play:** Have two players face each other (about 3 feet apart) in the middle of two safety lines which are marked approximately 30 feet behind each player, and place a poly spot between the two players along the center line. For multiple pairs, just space each pair a few feet apart along the center line and they also start by facing each other with a poly spot between them.

Designate one player as the "Odd" player and one as the "Even" player. Both players begin with one dice. On a "Go" signal, they each roll their dice toward the poly spot. The players immediately add the two numbers together which appear on the dice once they have come to a stop. If the answer is an even number, the "Even" player runs to his or her safety line; if the sum is an odd number, the "Odd" player runs to safety. The fleeing player gets a point if he or she makes it to the safety line without getting tagged. Likewise, the chasing player is credited with a point if he or she makes the tag before the safety line. After each turn, the players return to the middle and play again. The objective is to score as many points as possible.

As an alternative, consider having the players try multiplying or subtracting the two dice numbers to come up with a sum amount.

As a safety precaution, when playing with multiple pairs of players, emphasize the importance of running in a straight line back and forth between the safety lines. This will prevent players running into the area of other games being played.

Play is continuous until time is called.

# Partner Duck & Goose Tag

**Introduction:** The popular game of Duck, Duck, Goose is traditionally played with a large group. However, this modified version requires only two participants and requires much more movement. For a large group, have the players pair up and play multiple games simultaneously.

**Equipment:** Cones for marking safety lines, one poly spot for each pair of players

**How to Play:** Have two players face each other (about 3 feet apart) in the middle of two safety lines which are marked approximately 30 feet behind each player. Place a poly spot between the two players along the center line. For multiple pairs, space each pair a few feet apart along the center line and they also start by facing each other.

The two players begin by tapping each other on the shoulder and saying either "Duck" or "Goose." Neither player moves when "Duck" is said. However, when a player says "Goose," he or she turns with the other player in pursuit. The runner gets a point if he or she makes it to the safety line without getting tagged. Likewise, the chaser is credited with a point if he or she tags the runner before the safety line. After each turn, the players return to the middle and play again. The objective is to score as many points as possible.

As a safety precaution, when playing with multiple pairs of players, emphasize the importance of running in a straight between the safety lines. This will prevent players running into the area of other games being played.

Play is continuous until time is called.

# Partner Football Tag

**Introduction:** This "football game" enhances cardiovascular endurance while giving players an opportunity to practice hiking and catching a football. For a large group, just have the players find a partner and play multiple games simultaneously using a center line and two safety lines.

**Equipment:** One football for each pair of players; cones for marking safety lines, and one poly spot for each pair of players.

**How to Play:** Have two players stand (approximately 3 feet apart) and face each other in the middle of two safety lines which are marked approximately 30 feet behind each player. Place a poly spot between the two players along the center line. For multiple pairs, space each pair a few feet apart along the center line and they also begin by facing each other.

Designate one player as the "Quarterback," and the other as the "Hiker." The Hiker then takes the football and assumes the hiking position. The Quarterback, positioned about 5 feet behind the Hiker, says "Ready, Set, Hike!" The Hiker sends the football to the Quarterback on the "hike" signal. After catching the hiked ball, the Quarterback chases the Hiker to their safety line and attempts to make a tag with the football (no throwing is allowed). The Hiker gets a point if he or she makes it to safety line without getting tagged. Likewise, the Quarterback is credited with a point if he or she tags the runner before the safety line. After each turn, the players return to the middle, switch roles, and play again. The objective is to score as many points as possible.

As a safety precaution, when playing with multiple pairs of players, emphasize the importance of running in a straight line between the safety lines. This will prevent players from running into the area of other games being played.

Play is continuous until time is called.

# Partner Knee Tag

**Introduction:** This imaginative game resembles the sport of Fencing, in which partners try to score points by tagging each other—in this case, on the knees. For a large group, have all players find a partner and play multiple games simultaneously.

**Equipment:** None

**How to Play:** The players start by facing each other in a crouched position with right hands joined. For safety reasons, the hands have to stay joined throughout the game.

Using their free hand, the players attempt to tag either knee of the opponent, while at the same time, trying to keep their own knees from being tagged. Players can use a variety of circling and feinting movements before going for a quick tag to the knee, but they must keep their right hands joined at all times. Touching the knee with an open hand is the only type of touch allowed. Each successful tag counts as one point. The objective is to end with the highest number of points.

# Partner Math Tag

**Introduction:** This partner activity integrates math with the movement of playing tag. For a large group, have all players find a partner and play multiple games simultaneously using a center line and two safety lines.

**Equipment:** Cones for marking safety lines; one poly spot for each pair of players

**How to Play:** Have two players face each other (about 3 feet apart) in the middle of two safety lines (which are marked approximately 30 feet behind each player), and place a poly spot between the two players along the center line. For multiple pairs, space each pair a few feet apart along the center line and they will also start by facing each other with a poly spot between them.

Designate one player as the "More" player and one as the "Less" player. Both players begin with one hand behind their back, with all five fingers hidden from view. On a "Go" signal (the two players can alternate being the starter), they each hold out up to five fingers. If the sum of both partners' fingers is greater than five, the "More" player runs to his or her safety line. If the sum is five or less, the "Less" player runs to safety. The fleeing player gets a point if he or she makes it to the safety line without getting tagged. Likewise, the chasing player is credited with a point if he or she makes the tag before the safety line. After each turn, the players return to the middle and play again. The objective is to score as many points as possible.

As a safety precaution, when playing with multiple pairs of players, emphasize the importance of running in a straight line between the safety lines. This will prevent players from running into the area of other games being played.

Play is continuous until time is called.

# Partner Push-Up Tag

**Introduction:** With its circling, feinting, and quick movements, here's a fun tag game that is reminiscent of the one-on-one nature of individual sports such as Wrestling, Boxing, and Fencing. This activity is a terrific alternative to doing regular push-ups. For a large group, have players find a partner and play multiple games simultaneously.

**Equipment:** None

**How to Play:** The players start by facing each other about a foot apart in a push-up position. For safety reasons, remind the players to maintain some distance between them as to avoid any potential collisions.

Staying in the "up" position of a push-up, the players attempt to tag either hand of the opponent, while at the same time, trying to keep their own hands from being tagged. Players can use a variety of circling and feinting movements before going for a quick tag to the hand—but, but they must keep their knees off the floor at all times. Touching the hand with a light tap is the only type of touch allowed—no punching is allowed. Each successful tag counts as one point. The objective is to end with the highest number of points.

# Partner RPS Tag

**Introduction:** This version of "Rock-Paper-Scissors" requires only two participants and requires much more movement. For a large group, have players find a partner and play multiple games simultaneously using a center line and two safety lines.

**Equipment:** Cones for marking safety lines; one poly spot for each pair of players

**How to Play:** Have two players face each other (approximately 3 feet apart) in the middle of two safety lines which are marked approximately 30 feet behind each player. Place a poly spot between the two players along the center line. For multiple pairs, space each pair a few feet apart along the center line and they will also start by facing each other.

The two players begin by performing a rock-paper-scissors routine. A rock is a closed fist, paper is a flat hand, and scissors are the index and middle fingers in a cutting position. Paper always covers rock, rock beats scissors, and scissors cut paper. To determine a winner, the players count to three and form a rock, paper, or scissors. The winning player then chases the losing player toward his or her safety line attempting to make a tag. The losing player gets a point if he or she makes it to the safety line without getting tagged. Likewise, the chaser (or winning player) is credited with a point if he or she makes the tag before the safety line. After each turn, the players return to the middle and play again. The objective is to score as many points as possible.

As a safety precaution, when playing with multiple pairs of players, emphasize the importance of running in a straight line between the safety lines. This will prevent players running into the area of other games being played.

Play is continuous until time is called.

# Partner Toe Tag

**Introduction:** With its circling, feinting, and quick movements, here's a fun tag game that is reminiscent of the one-on-one nature of Fencing. For a large group, have players find a partner and play multiple games simultaneously.

**Equipment:** None

**How to Play:** The players start by facing each other in a crouched position with the hands placed on the shoulders of the other player. For safety reasons, the hands have to stay on the opponent's shoulders throughout the game.

Using only feet, the players attempt to tag either foot of the opponent, while at the same time, trying to keep their own feet from being tagged. Players can use a variety of circling and feinting movements before going for a quick tag to the foot—but, they must keep their hands on each other's shoulders at all times. Touching the foot with a light tap is the only type of touch allowed—no kicking or stomping is allowed. Each successful tag counts as one point. The objective is to end with the highest number of points.

# Bunny Hop Dance Tag

**Introduction:** This game integrates the playing of tag using the steps performed in the "Bunny Hop" dance. This is a great activity for younger players as it allows the practicing of the dance steps in a setting which is done cooperatively with one person at a time—at a level and pace of their choosing.

**Equipment:** Several player identification vests or foam balls for the taggers

**How to Play:** Before play, spend time practicing the steps of the "Bunny Hop" dance.

Select several players to be the chasers and hand each an identification vest or foam ball for tagging. The remaining players start scattered around the play area.

On a starting signal, the chasers attempt to tag the other players. Once tagged, players must freeze in a standing position with one hand held high. Tagged players can be set free when a free player approaches and together they perform one round of the "Bunny Hop" dance. No rescuing player can be tagged while performing the Bunny Hop.

Play is continuous. Select new chasers often.

# Chicken Dance Tag

**Introduction:** This favorite game enhances cardiovascular endurance and rhythmic skills by integrating the playing of tag with the steps used in the "Chicken Dance."

**Equipment:** Several player identification vests or foam balls for the taggers

**How to Play:** Before play, spend time practicing the steps of the "Chicken Dance."

Select several players to be the chasers and hand each one an identification vest or foam ball for tagging. The remaining players start scattered around the play area.

On a starting signal, the chasers attempt to tag the other players. Once tagged, players must freeze in a standing position with one hand held high. Tagged players can be set free when a free player approaches and together they perform one round of the "Chicken Dance." No rescuing player can be tagged while performing the Chicken Dance.

Play is continuous. Select new chasers often.

# 60's Dance Tag

**Introduction:** This is a great way to combine the music and dance of the 1960's, with the fun of playing tag. Using the music of Chubby Checker and dancing to his popular song, "Twist," is a great introduction to the dances of that era.

**Equipment:** Several player identification vests or foam balls for the taggers

**How to Play:** Before play, spend time practicing the steps of the "Twist" dance (or any of the popular dances performed from the 1960's). Since "twisting" is a simple move, this game can be used by children of all ages.

Select several players to be the chasers and hand each one an identification vest or foam ball for tagging. The remaining players start scattered around the play area.

On a starting signal, the chasers attempt to tag the other players. Once tagged, players must freeze in a standing position with one hand held high. Tagged players can be set free when a free player approaches and together they perform several rounds of the "Twist" dance. No rescuing player can be tagged while performing the Twist.

Play is continuous. Select new chasers often.

# Square Dance Tag

**Introduction:** This game enhances both cardiovascular endurance and rhythmic skills by combining the game of tag with common square dancing steps.

**Equipment:** Several player identification vests or foam balls for the taggers

**How to Play:** Before play, spend time practicing various square dance steps, such as the partner swing, do-si-do, allemande right/left, and so forth.

Select several players to be the chasers and hand each one an identification vest or foam ball for tagging. The remaining players start scattered around the play area.

On a starting signal, the chasers attempt to tag the other players. Once tagged, players must freeze in a standing position with one hand held high. Tagged players can be set free when a free player approaches and together they perform one round of a specific square dance movement (this can be any of those mentioned above). No rescuing player can be tagged while performing a square dance step.

Play is continuous. Select new chasers often.

# Swing Dance Tag

**Introduction:** This game enhances both cardiovascular endurance and rhythmic skills by mixing swing dance steps with the active movement of playing tag. This game is especially fun to play with swing dance music playing in the background.

**Equipment:** Several player identification vests or foam balls for the taggers

**How to Play:** Before play, spend time practicing the various steps used in the East Coast Swing, Charleston, Lindy Hop, and so forth. For younger players, simply use a modified version of any of the above.

Select several players to be the chasers and hand each one an identification vest or foam ball for tagging. The remaining players start scattered around the play area.

On a starting signal, the chasers attempt to tag the other players. Once tagged, players must freeze in a standing position with one hand held high. Tagged players can be set free when a free player approaches and together they cooperatively perform one round of a specific swing dance movement. No rescuing player can be tagged while performing a swing dance step.

Play is continuous. Select new chasers often.

# YMCA Dance Tag

**Introduction:** This game integrates the playing of tag with the arm movements used in the "YMCA" dance. This game is especially fun with the song "YMCA," by the Village People, playing in the background.

**Equipment:** Several player identification vests or foam balls for the taggers

**How to Play:** Before play, spend time practicing the arm movements used in the "YMCA" dance.

Select several players to be the chasers and hand each one an identification vest or foam ball for tagging. The remaining players start scattered around the play area.

On a starting signal, the chasers attempt to tag the other players. Once tagged, players must freeze in a standing position with one hand held high. Tagged players can be set free when a free player approaches and together they perform one round of the arm movements used in the "YMCA" dance. No rescuing player can be tagged while performing the "YMCA" dance.

Play is continuous. Select new chasers often.

Made in the USA
San Bernardino, CA
16 October 2013